I0845905

Preface

Drawing has always been a way for me to explore new ideas, and this book represents some of those ideas that I've transformed from concepts into visual representations over the past few years.
As a designer, the ability to visualise what my mind creates is as important as choosing the right words when communicating with others.

This book serves as an exercise in projecting my most complex ideas into drawings, containing illustrations that I've attempted to create almost daily. These drawings combine elements from fantastical realms, nature, architecture, and other themes that have long held my interest.

As you peruse these pages, you'll witness how my drawings have evolved, with increasing levels of detail and my continual efforts to push the boundaries of what I want to depict by infusing stories and context. I invite you to step into this world where creativity reigns, distractions fade, and art becomes the only storyline. So, turn the page, take a deep breath, and join me on a journey of introspection into my creative universe.

In this book, I'm sharing my illustrations with you not as a professional designer, but as someone who seeks peace and clarity through art to inspire others to discover what brings them peace and creativity.

A tale told through drawings

Nirvana

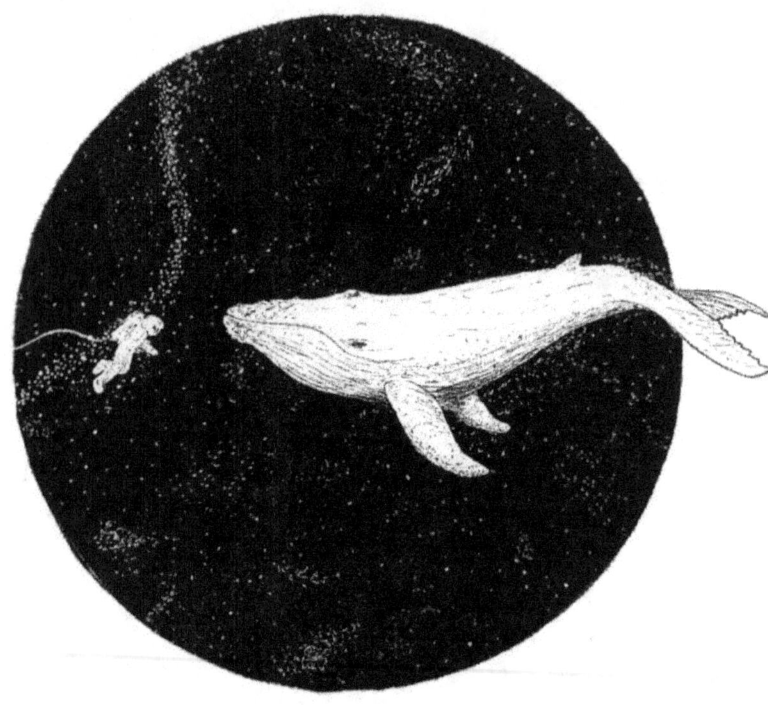

Imagine the deepest of dives, exploring the vastness of the universe in search of something new, never seen before, and finding one of the quietest creatures in the silence.

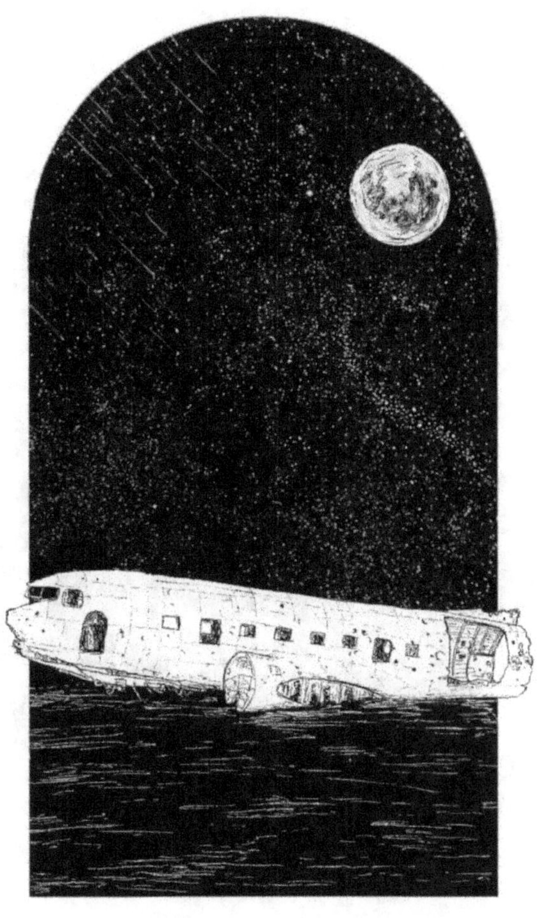

What was once a machine that sailed the skies now rests quietly on the shores of the land of ice and fire, spending its time following the changes in the tide and witnessing the longest days and nights. It waits for the final moment when decay takes complete control.

Evolve

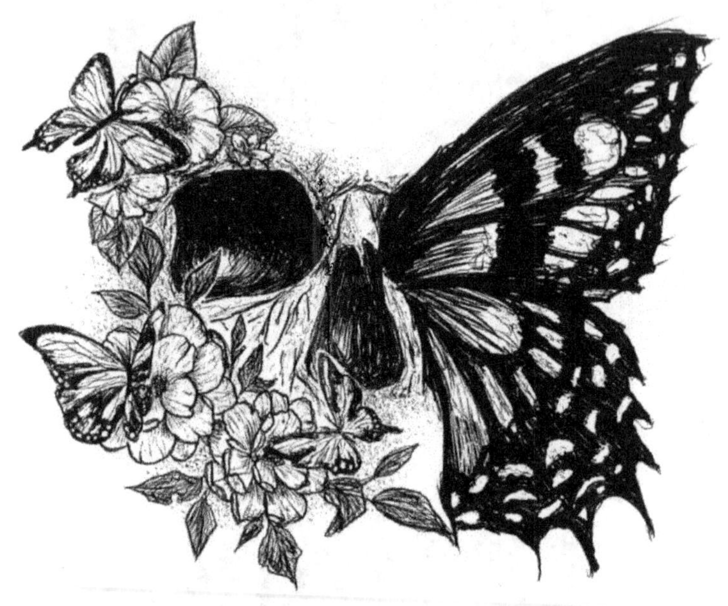

Nature taking over life, when time doesn't stop
and the eternal creation keeps evolving its
environment, there's nothing to do other than to
exist, living in the moment, and whatever
happens will happen.

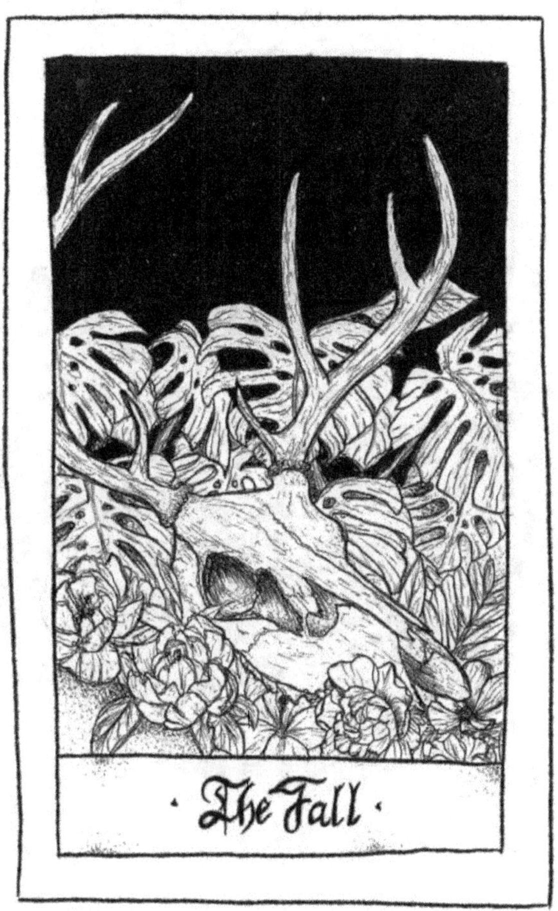

A reminder that all things come to an end, much like a tarot card depicting the future. With "The Tall," it signifies the ultimate conclusion, that regardless of our actions in life, we all arrive at the same destination, making way for others to flourish.

Vagabond

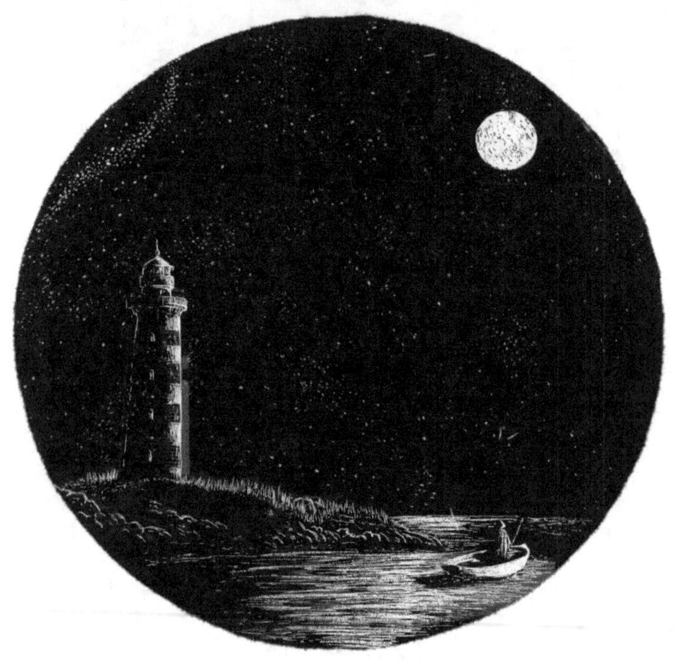

The traveler, akin to an aimless wanderer, steers through the seas guided solely by the moonlight, the stars, and the intermittent beacon of a lighthouse situated in a land unknown to them, yet brimming with potential for discovery.

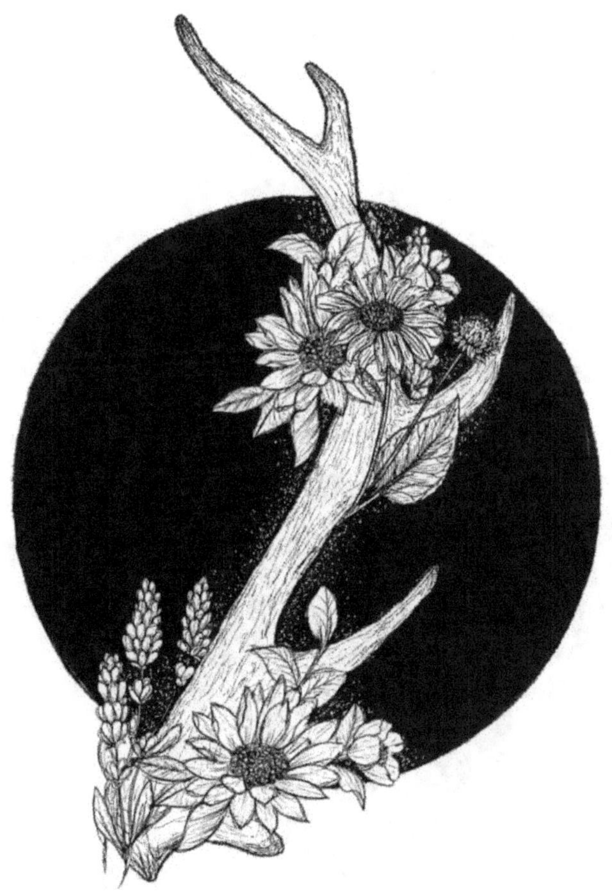

Nature always finds a way, and the comfort of what once held life provides the best foundation for setting roots. Flourishing in the most unexpected places, like the peace we all seek, or the guidance needed to grow bigger and stronger.

The Last Call

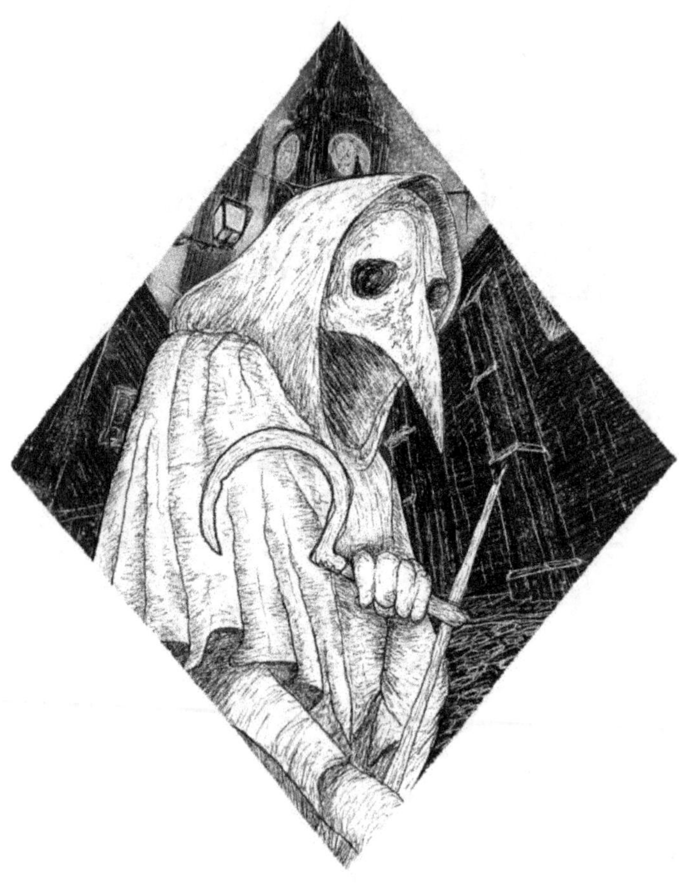

In the middle of the darkest night, walking around
the quiet streets of London, there's a silent killer
wandering the streets and nobody is safe from it,
only time will tell until the last of those hidden prevail
to see the light of another day.

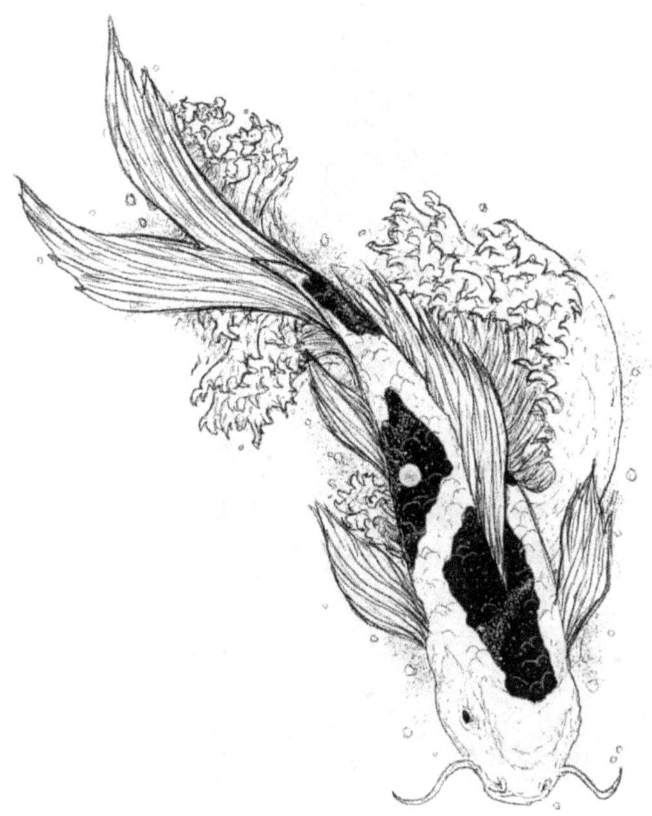

Flowing through the currents, navigating the uncertainties of life, and embracing every wave, it effortlessly propels itself forward, fearless of what lies ahead. Sensing every change in the water's flow, it adjusts its direction to avoid disruption to its course.

Whisper

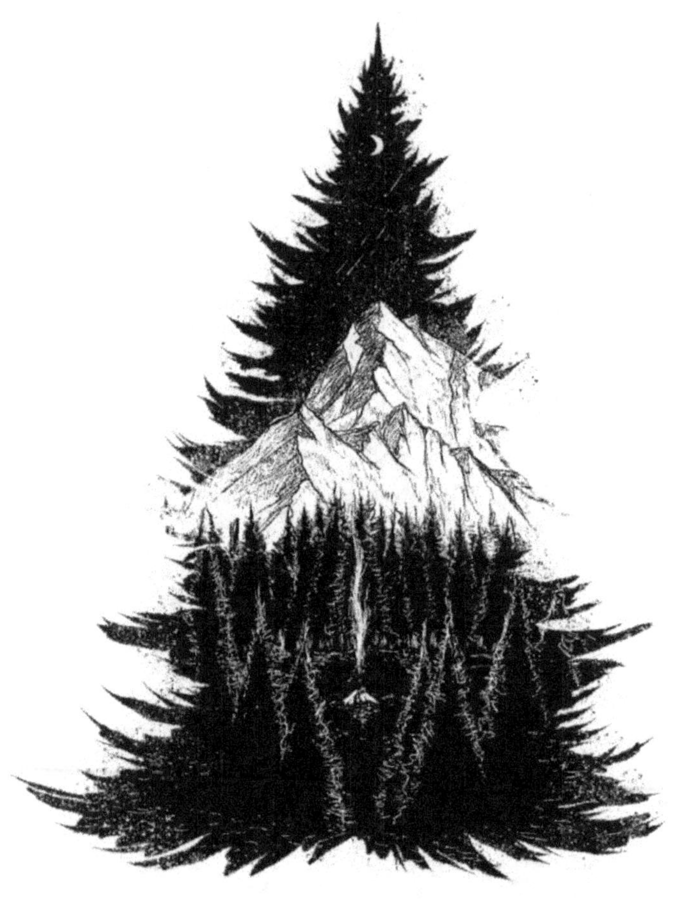

Imagine the deepest of dives, exploring the vastness of the universe in search of something new, never seen before, and finding one of the quietest creatures in the silence.

Liftoff

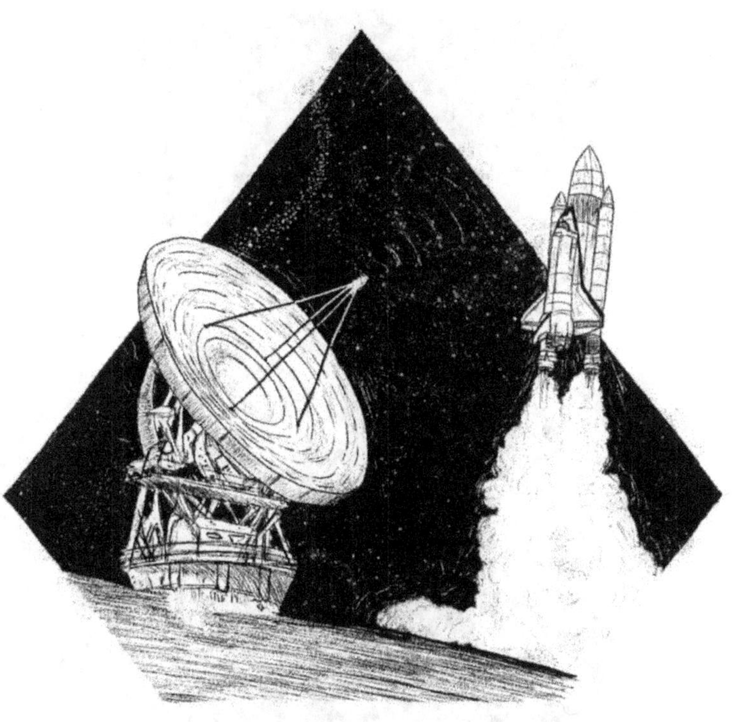

Mission control gives the go-ahead, everything is quiet, the spark that lights everything up goes on and in seconds it's already on its way. Blasting off sound and smoke, creating a pillar of ballistic sonic noise, it aims for the place unreachable before.

Running

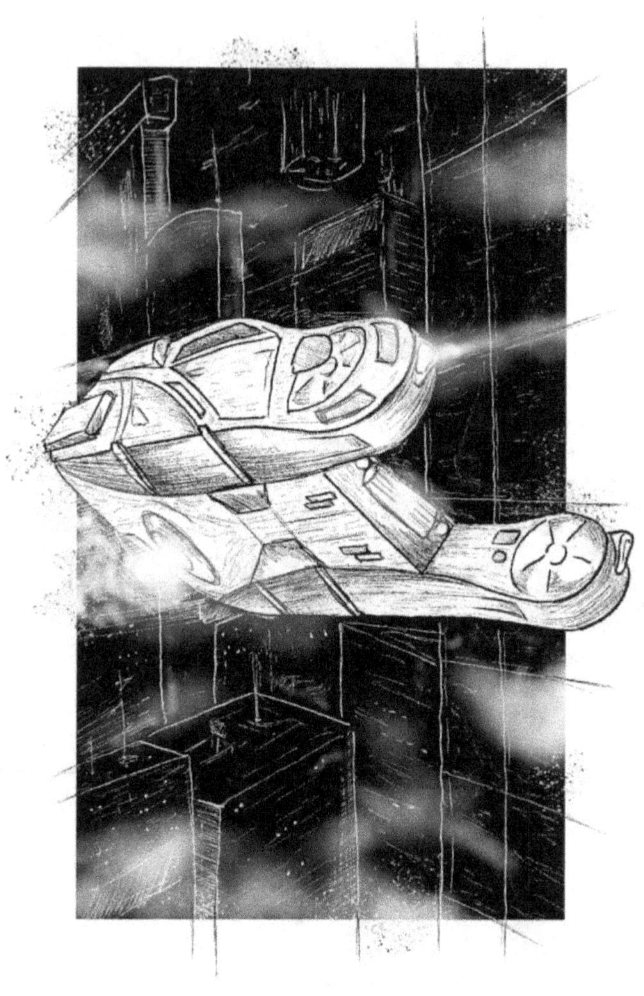

Neon nights and smoky alleys, with noise and loud music emanating from every open window. The rush of a restless city, where eternal nights guide the time. A land with no rules, where every second counts – live or let live, but always leave a mark.

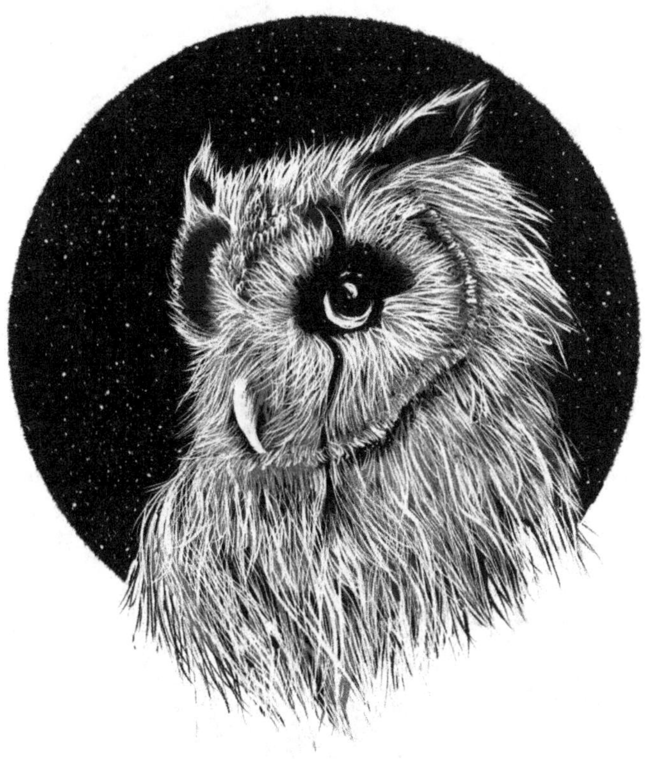

Like a view into the stars, a quiet owl awaits its pray
in the darkness of the night, and his sight is just the
darkest dark, until the most subtle of the movements
disturb the silent in time for an attack.

Prism

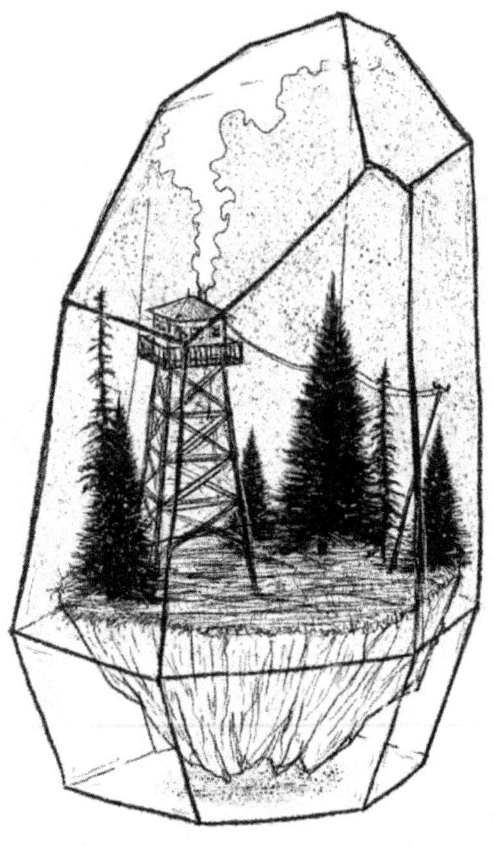

In a land constrained by space, the fire watch remains vigilant, protecting the surrounding nature. They acknowledge that silence often signifies safety, with the only audible cracks being those of animals roaming in the undergrowth.

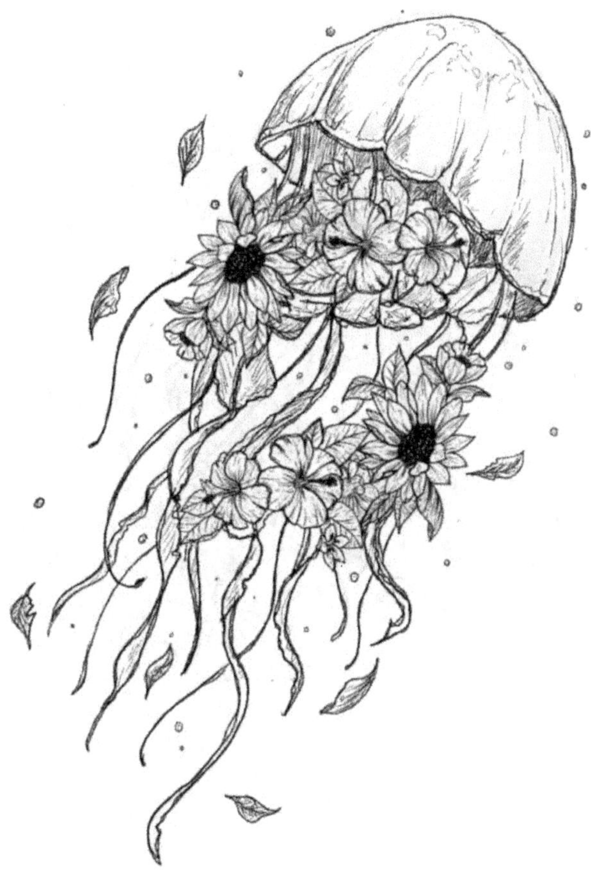

Amid a vast emptiness of floating leaves, a delicate jellyfish drifts, its ethereal form a stark contrast to the stillness of its surroundings. In this pristine realm, where silence reigns and nature thrives, the creature glides serenely, a shimmering beacon of graceful existence.

Arcadia

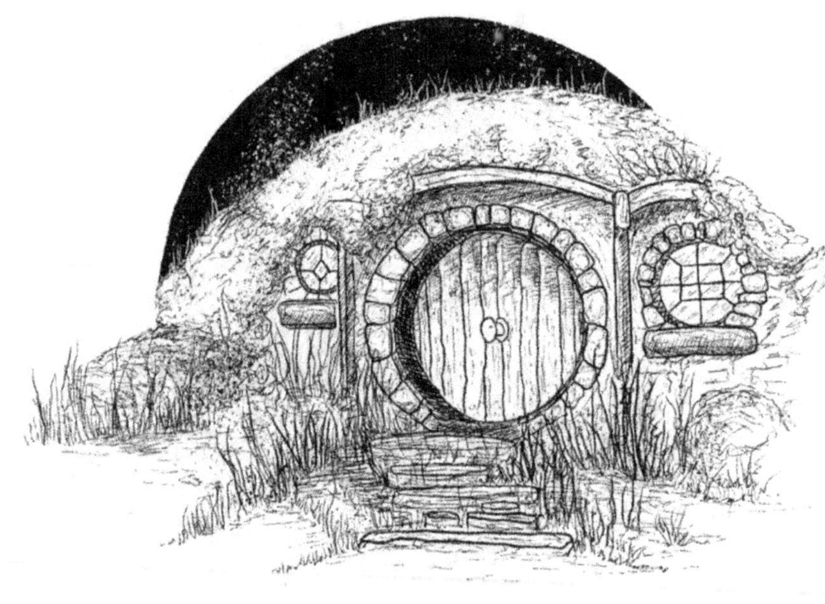

The entrance to a hole in the ground, home to a thousand stories and quaint delights. A pastel door, a leaf-shaped knocker, and a round doorknob exude rustic charm. Coziness welcomes visitors, eagerly anticipating endless adventures.

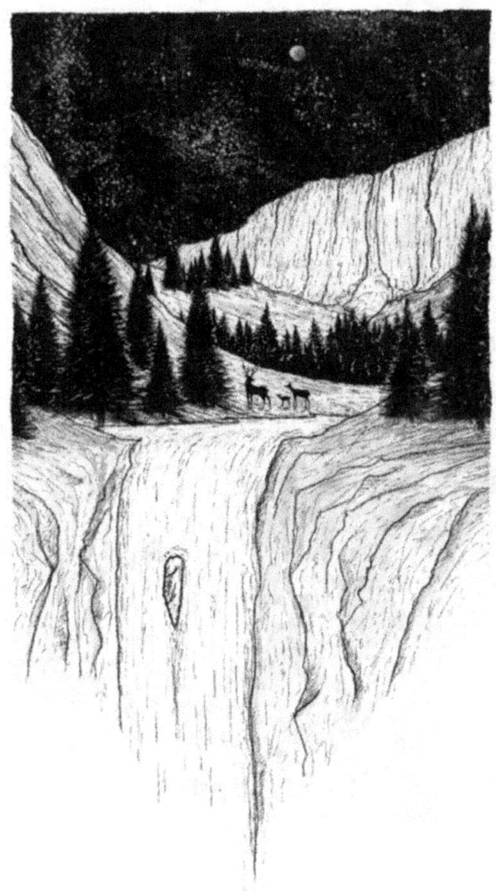

Amid the tranquil night's darkness, a serene tableau emerges. In the heart of a lush valley, a majestic waterfall cascades, its silvery streams glistening in the moonlight. The hush beckons creatures to approach the water, enticing them to savour the bounties of nature.

Vessel

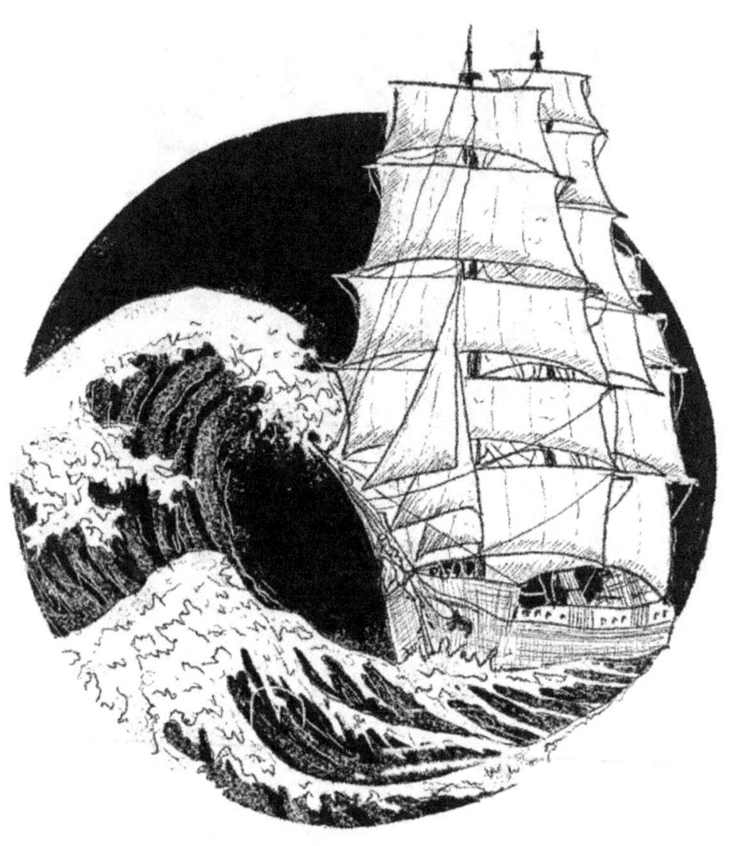

In a nocturnal spectacle of water, wind and hectic torrents, a fearless sailing vessel plunges headlong into a raging sea under the shroud of night. Towering waves, like monstrous apparitions, rear up to challenge the ship's direction.

Last Dive

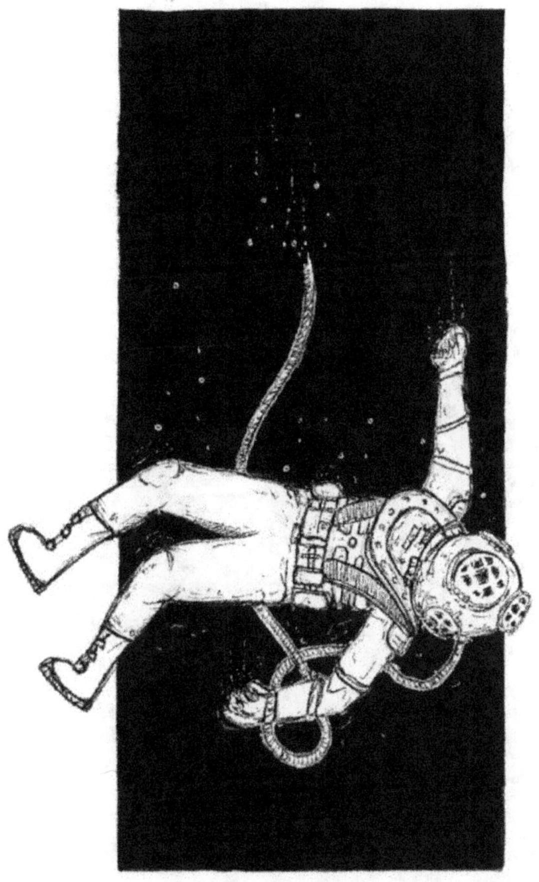

Chaos, darkness and lifeless currents frame the last breaths of an explorer unaware of what was ahead of them. Abyssal creatures await in the bed of the water, where out of control and without being able to return home will end up becoming their gravestone.

Sour

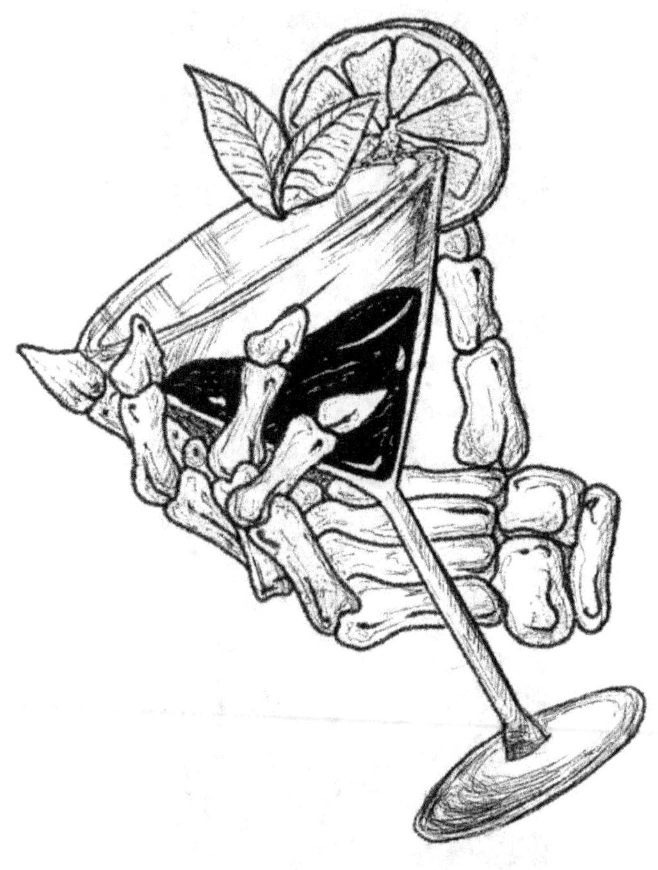

Lifeless nights of music, loud echoes in the night call for the party to continue while a never-ending flow of liquor gives flavour and smell to the spirits that gather to celebrate the end of time, with just a song after another and no more worries in mind.

Dumbo

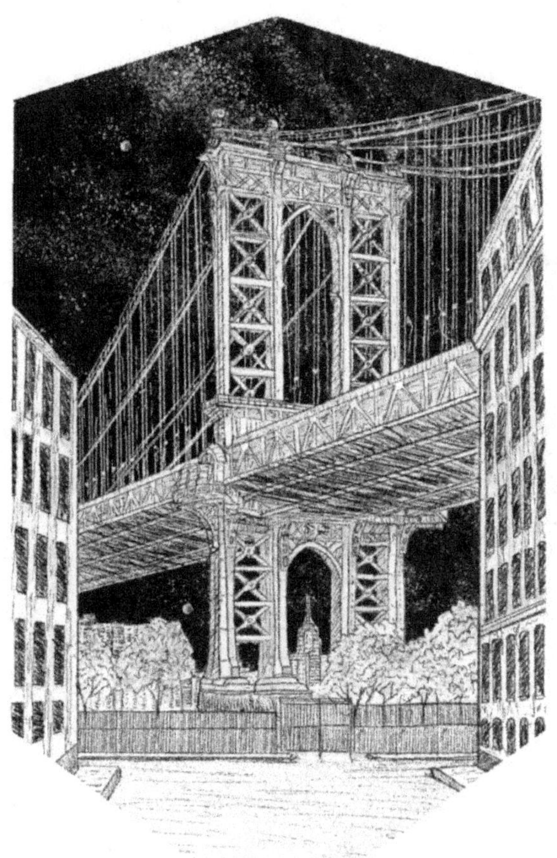

Roads of cobblestone, concrete giants roaming the land, settling and standing tall observing flow of passersby walking aimlessly in the middle of the chaos, while the iron mammoth stands by, from the distance, motionless over time but being noticed by everyone around it.

The Hunt

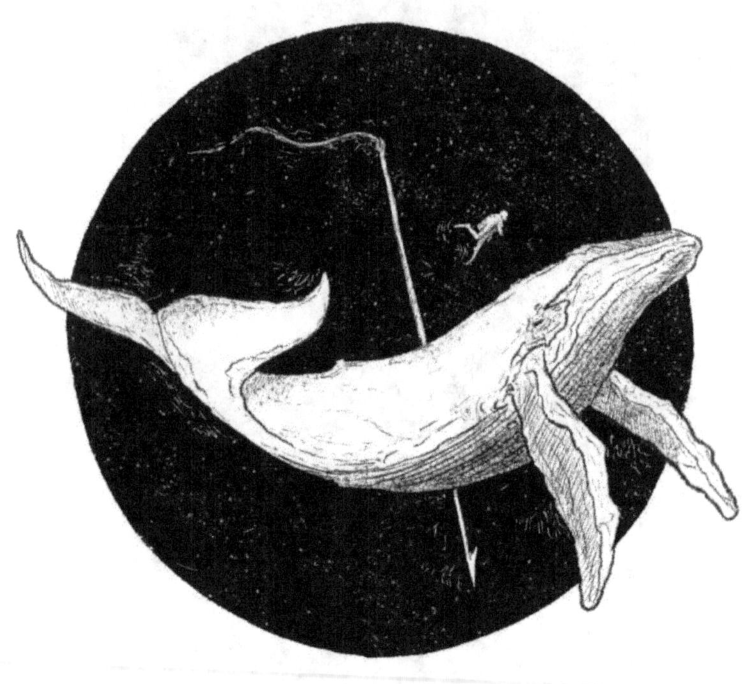

Beneath the waves, a world of silence unfolds. In
the depths of the ocean, the prey flows ahead,
gliding majestically through the dark waters,
followed by its savior or hunter, reaching to
confront an inevitable end.

Time

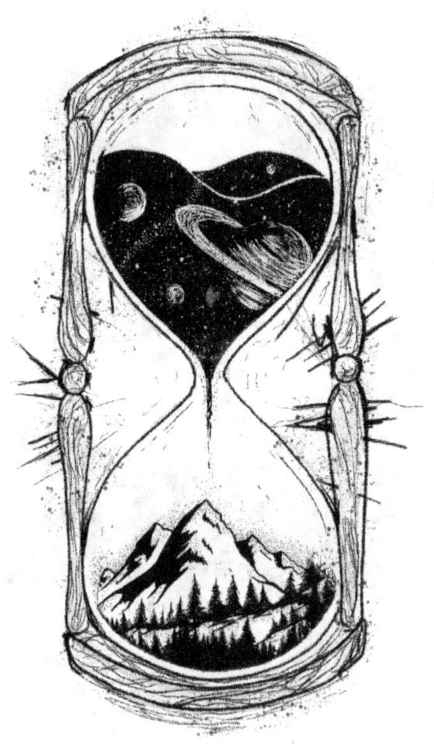

In the grand cosmic theater, time doesn't wait, and the cascade evokes the present moment. The grains of stardust, resembling a mesmerizing cosmic river, flow inexorably downward, measuring the passage of eons in their descent towards the present.

Moonshine

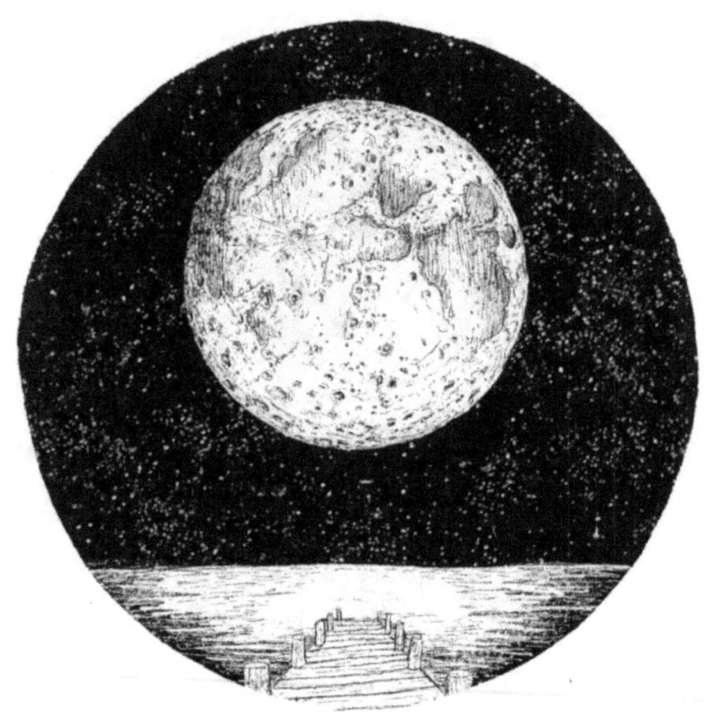

Beneath the velvety night sky, a tranquil lake mirrors the enchanting vision of a colossal moon, its silvery glow casting a serene radiance upon the calm waters, inviting quiet contemplation beneath the celestial masterpiece.

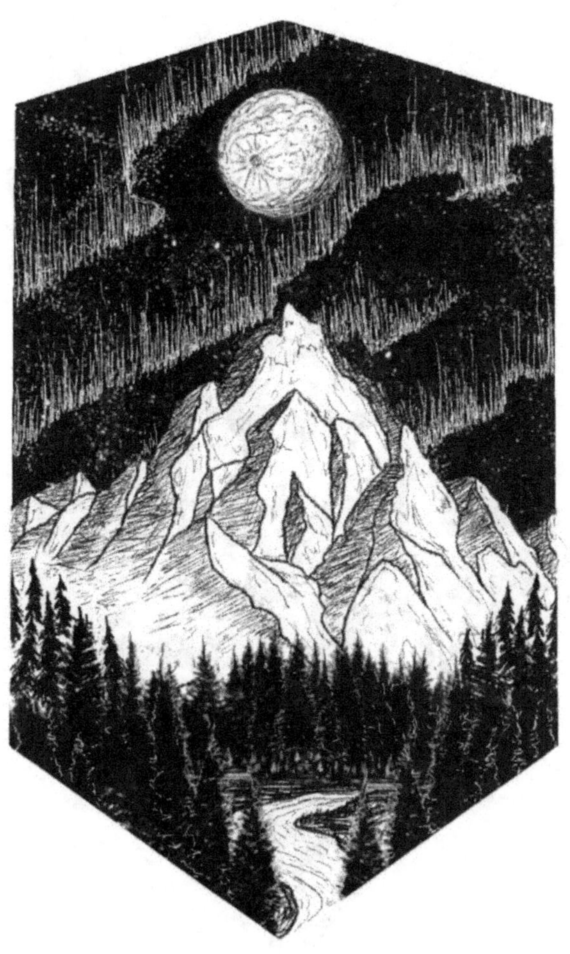

In the serene night, a valley cradles a winding river,
embraced by towering mountains and a forest. Above, the
northern lights weave their luminous magic in a tranquil,
natural tableau. There's only silence with the mute
whisper of the trees moving by the blowing of the wind.

Observant

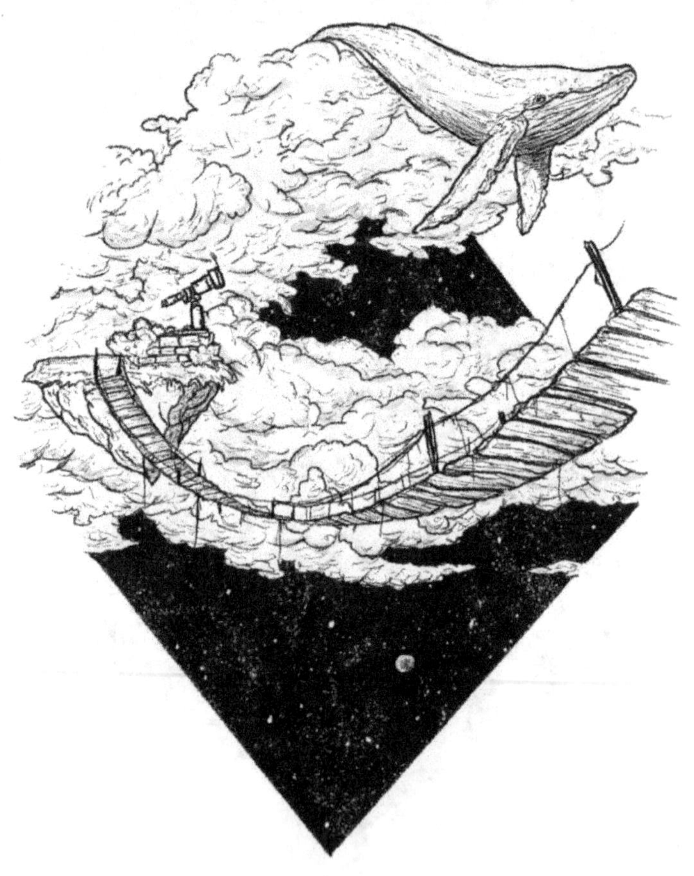

Amongst the celestial clouds, a surreal vision unfolds. A colossal whale soars through the skies, accompanied by an observation post perched atop a cloud. The skyward reverie protects the skies from dangers.

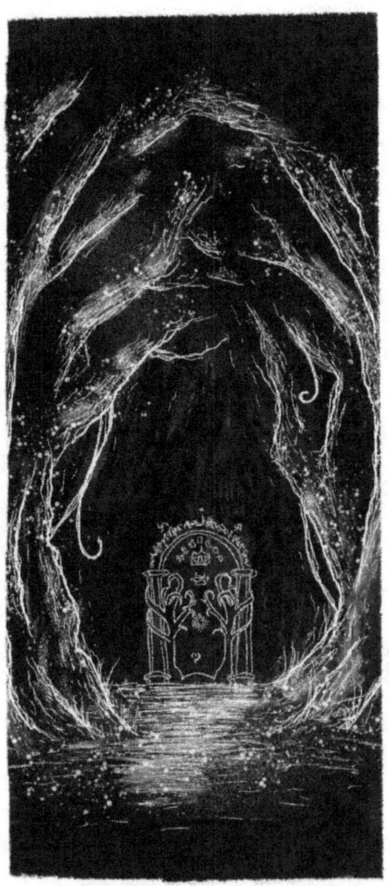

Amid the hushed stillness of the night, the concealed entrance to Moria, the Doors of Durin, bursts forth in radiant light between the sentinel trees. Awaiting for adventures, ready to let the explorers in, awaits restful with the mesmerising light inviting the curious to peak inside.

Vagabond

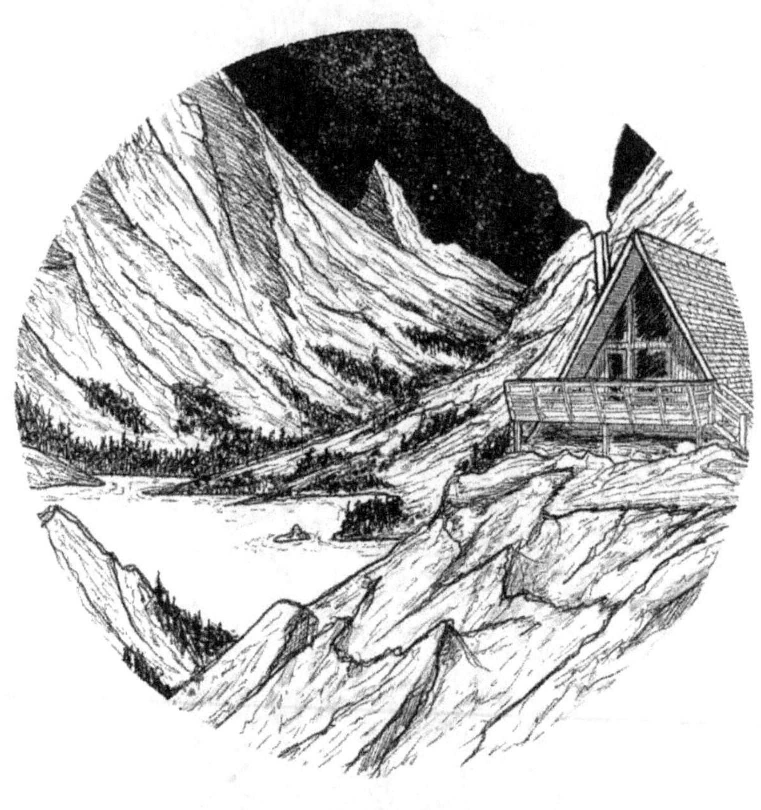

In the moonlit mountain wilderness, a solitary cabin
perches above the valley. Its occupant, much like an
aimless wanderer, seeks the silent embrace of the night,
guided only by moonlight and stars, surrounded by
untapped potential.

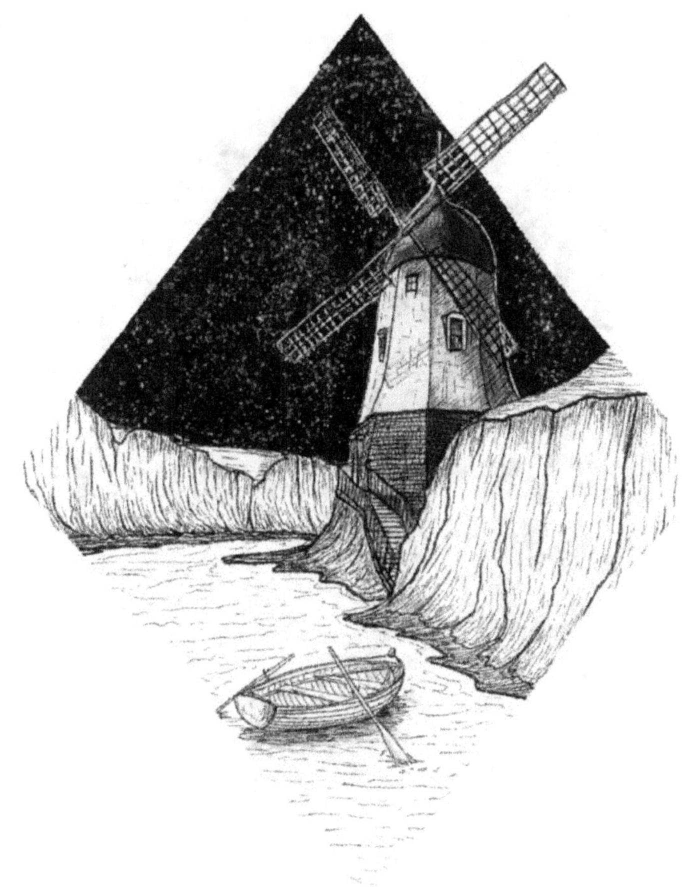

In the moonlit coastal scene, cliffs rise along the shore, accompanied by a windmill spinning in the night breeze. As a boat approaches, the tranquil beauty evokes a sense of calm, standing as a mirage in the stillness of the evening.

Passive

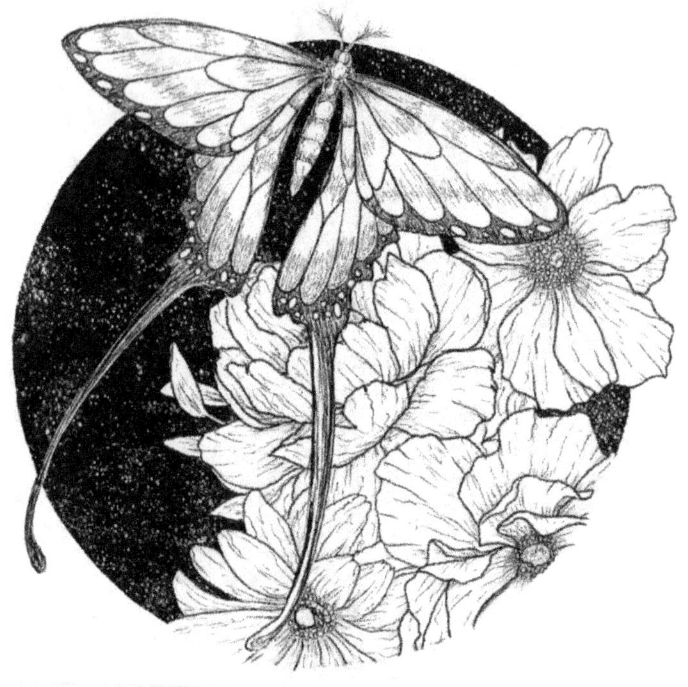

Nestled in a garden, a delicate butterfly gently reclines
upon vivid blossoms. It savors the tranquil rhythm of
time passing by, a serene witness to nature's
ever-changing tapestry. With grace, it finds solace in
the stillness, embracing each fleeting moment,

Breakwater

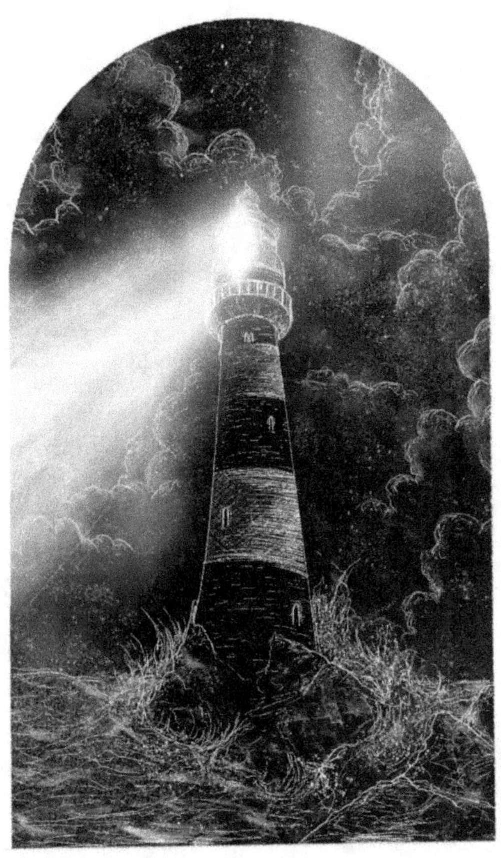

Amidst the tumultuous sea on a tempestuous night, a resolute lighthouse stands sentinel upon a rugged, wave-battered breakwater. Its beam pierces the darkness, guiding ships safely through the chaos, a symbol of unwavering strength and hope in the face of nature's fury.

Outbound

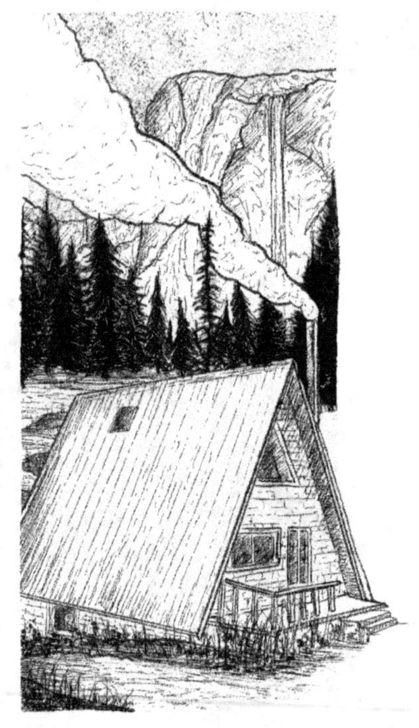

In the tranquil solitude of a winter's day, a cozy cabin stands by a frozen lake, encircled by snow-covered peaks and silent woods. A distant waterfall adds its voice to nature's serene lullaby making it the guardian of the valley.

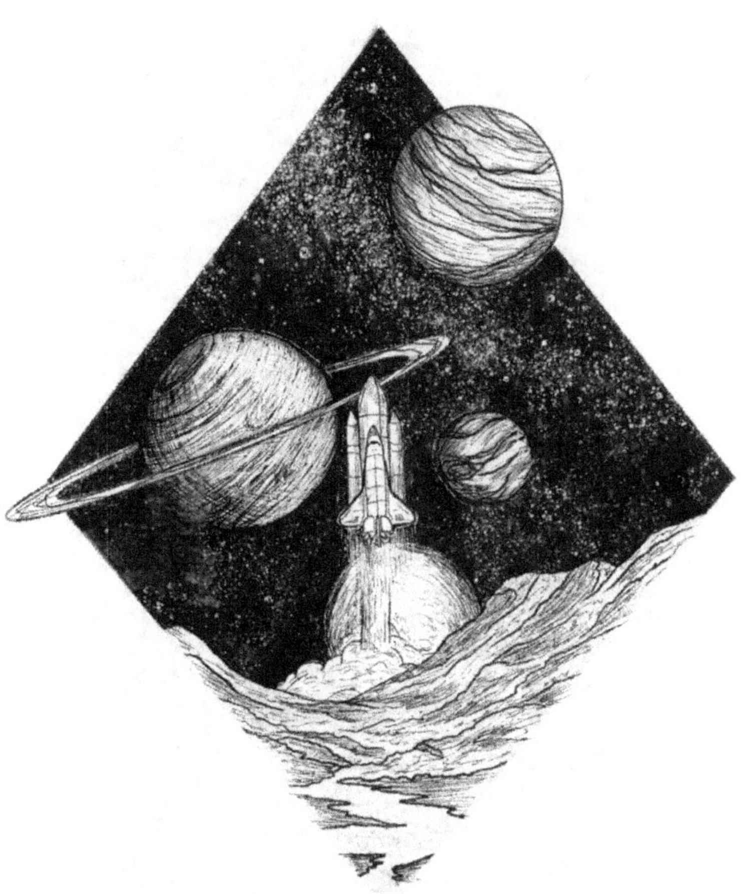

As the day fades on an alien world, a spaceship readies for its journey. Against a celestial backdrop of shimmering stars and planetary bodies, it gracefully ascends, embarking on an odyssey to explore the boundless wonders of the universe.

Endless

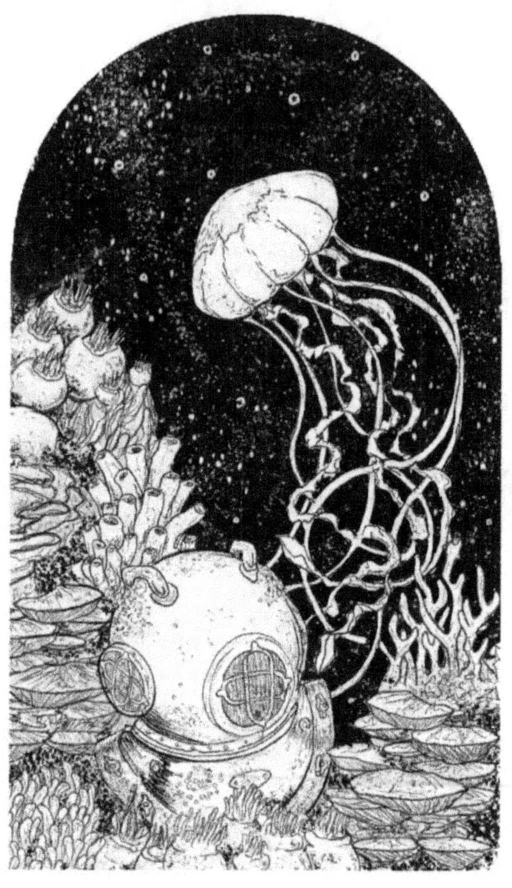

In the eerie beauty of the abyss, a majestic jellyfish, with tendrils swaying like ethereal banners, navigates the mysterious depths. Amid remnants of a diver's suit and a thriving coral reef, it epitomizes the timeless allure of the undersea world.

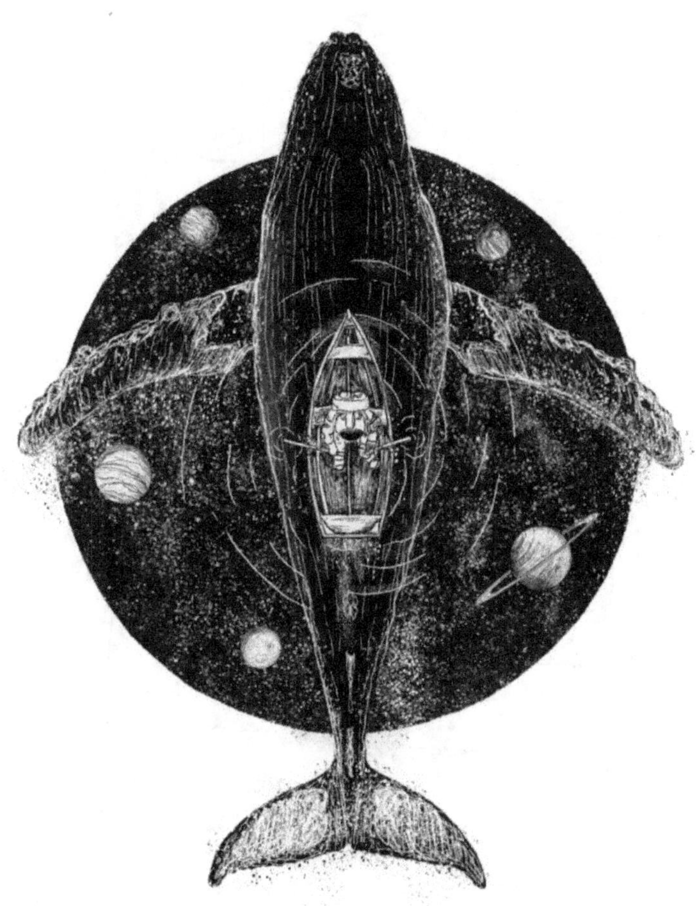

An astronaut embarks on a cosmic voyage, drifting silently in a small boat through the universe like a lost sailor. Beneath, a majestic whale glides through the celestial sea, unnoticed where they flow aimlessness to the depths of the unknown.

New Utopia

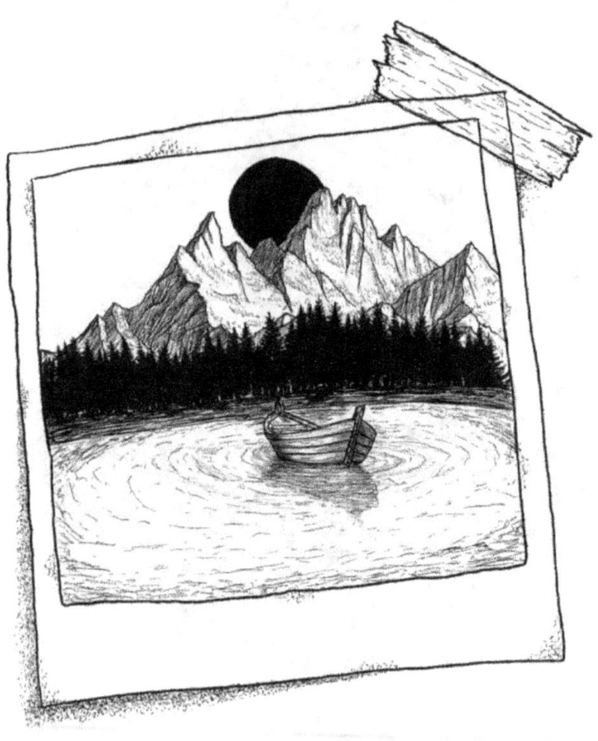

Postcards of a new world, capturing what a could be an everlasting scene of a peaceful landscape. Reflections of a new, golden light warm up the scene creating a haven of tranquil beauty in the natural world, and a restful vessel awaits for its new adventure.

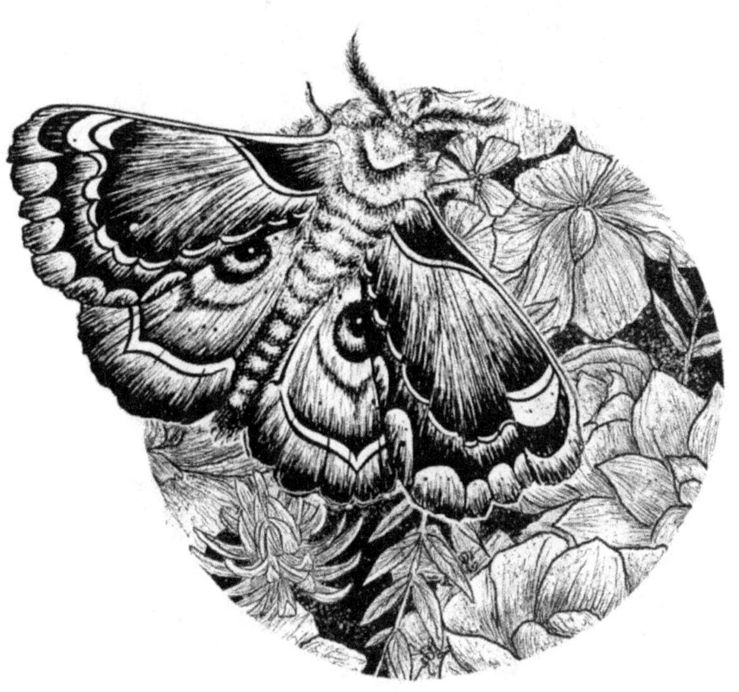

Amidst the gentle sway of blossoms, a solitary moth graces the scene with its graceful flight, as if painting poetry in the air. It hovers, a symbol of delicate elegance, embracing the serenity of nature, poised in patient anticipation of its forthcoming nourishment.

Earthbound

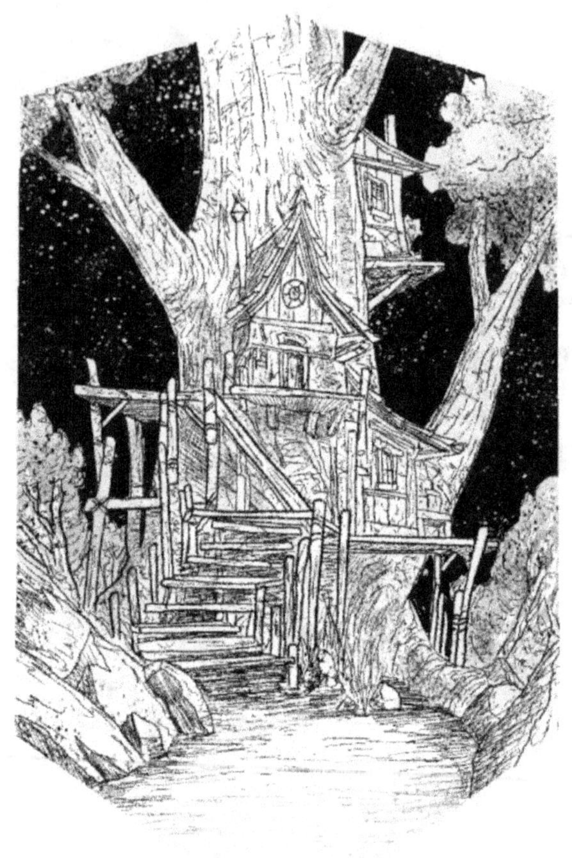

Nestled in ancient woods, a dwelling emerges within a colossal tree trunk, a harmonious testament to human ingenuity and nature's grandeur. This rustic abode blends imagination and organic architecture, bridging humanity with the woodland's venerable embrace.

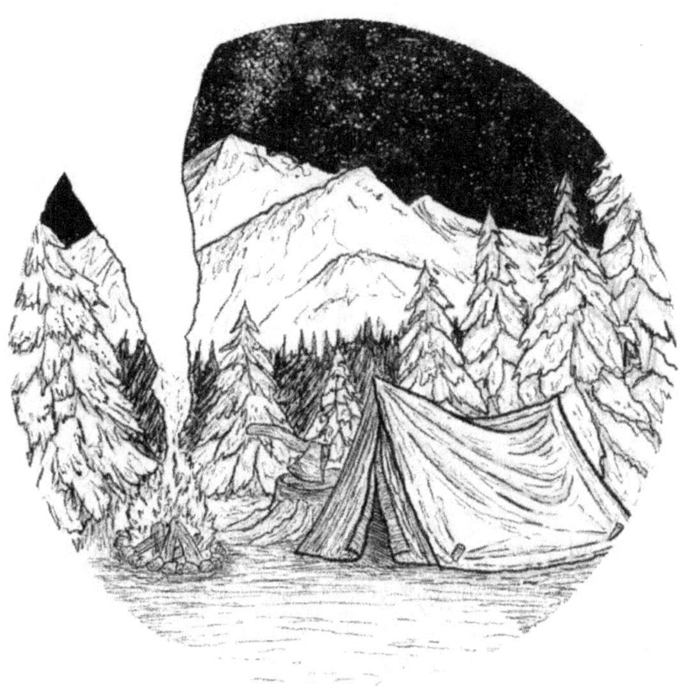

Within the heart of the sprawling forest, an isolated tent emerges. Encircled by a small fire, it stands as an inviting focal point, a place where stories and secrets are bound to be told amid the captivating flames, surrounded by the wild embrace of nature.